From Milk to Ice Cream

From Milk to Ice Cream

Ali Mitgutsch

 Carolrhoda Books, Inc., Minneapolis

First published in the United States of America 1981 by
Carolrhoda Books, Inc. All English language rights reserved.

Original edition © 1979 by Sellier Verlag GmbH, Eching bei München,
West Germany, under the title VON DER MILCH ZUM SPEISEEIS.
Revised English text © 1981 by Carolrhoda Books, Inc.
Illustrations © 1979 by Sellier Verlag GmbH.

Manufactured in the United States of America.

LIBRARY OF CONGRESS CATALOGING IN PUBLICATION DATA

Mitgutsch, Ali.
  From milk to ice cream.

    (A Carolrhoda start to finish book)
    Edition for 1979 published under title: Von der Milch
zum Speiseeis.
    SUMMARY: Describes how ice cream is made from
milk.

    1. Ice cream, ices, etc.—Juvenile literature. [1. Ice
cream, ices, etc.] I. Title.

TX795.M7313   1981   637'.4   81-82
ISBN 0-87614-158-0 (lib. bdg.)   AACR1
ISBN 0-87614-465-2 (pbk.)

    3 4 5 6 7 8 9 10 97 96 95 94 93 92 91 90 89 88 87

From Milk
to Ice Cream

Ice cream is made from milk.

Most of the milk we use comes from cows.

To make ice cream, sugar is added to the milk.

They are mixed together in a large machine.

This machine heats the mixture

and then quickly cools it.

This kills any germs that might be in it.

Then all the lumps in the mixture are broken up

so it is very smooth.

The mixture now looks like thick paste.

Now it is time to add the flavoring.
Ingredients for flavoring ice cream
come from all over the world.
They come by ship, truck, and plane.

Some of the things used for flavoring ice cream are nuts, cocoa, fruit, and coffee.

The flavoring is stirred into the sugar-milk paste.

Then the paste is pressed through a round tube.

As it comes out of this tube,

the paste is cut into pieces.

The pieces of ice cream paste drop into containers,

and the containers are sealed.

The cartons of ice cream paste
now go through a cold tunnel.
This tunnel is a freezer
where the paste freezes into ice cream.

Then the cartons of ice cream are packed
and loaded into refrigerator trucks.
These trucks are like giant freezers.
They will keep the ice cream frozen
while it is being delivered.

The ice cream is taken to stores, restaurants, and ice cream parlors, ready for us to enjoy.

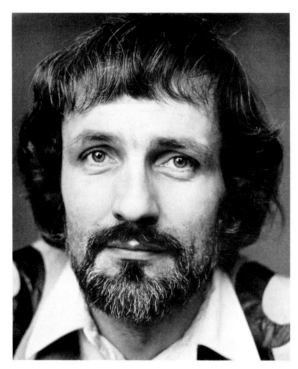

Ali
Mitgutsch

ALI MITGUTSCH is one of Germany's best-known children's book illustrators. He is a devoted world traveler, and many of his book ideas have taken shape during his travels. Perhaps this is why they have such international appeal. Mr. Mitgutsch's books have been published in 22 countries and are enjoyed by thousands of readers around the world.

Ali Mitgutsch lives with his wife and three children in Schwabing, the artists' quarter in Munich. The Mitgutsch family also enjoys spending time on their farm in the Bavarian countryside.

# THE CAROLRHODA
>>> START

TO FINISH >>>
BOOKS